RUN IN SUCH A WAY

Training for Life in the Kingdom of God

Run to the King Prakin!

Tom

Tom Houser

Run in Such a Way
Copyright © 2015 by Tom Houser

ISBN 978-1511932646

Cover design: Ryan Smith
Cover photo: CT Photomemories (ctphotomemories.com)

Printed in the United States of America

This book is dedicated to Jim Zuber. God used Jim in my life in many ways, but one in particular continues to affect me. He taught a very simple spiritual disciplines class at Linworth Road Community Church in Worthington, Ohio. This class showed me that the *Spirit of God* can use the *Word of God* to transform *people of God* into the *image of God*.

Jim was the man God used to flip my spiritual switch from *OFF* to *ON*. I have never been the same.

Do you not know that in a race all the runners run, but only one gets the prize?
Run in such a way as to get the prize.

1 Corinthians 9:24 (NIV)

Contents

.

Introduction

When I pick up a book, I always wonder if I will finish it. Will it draw me in? Will it be interesting? Will it help me understand something better or do something differently? In essence, I'm asking this question: "Is this book worth my time?"

You may be wondering the same thing: *Is this book worth my time?* And that is a totally legitimate question. To help you answer that question, I'll ask you to spend 60 seconds considering these questions:

> *Would you like to know Jesus at a deep, personal level?*
>
> *Would you like to have real, lasting peace and joy?*
>
> *Would you like to have a heart that overflows with love for God and people?*
>
> *Would you like to be set free from greed? Pride? Lust? Anger? Deceit? Fear?*

Would you like to be the kind of person that is learning to trust God more and more?

Would you like to live the kind of life that honors God, even in the little things?

Would you like to be part of a community of people that wants these same things?

Oh, and here's one more question:

Do you think God wants these things for you?

If you answered 'yes' to some of these questions, this book will be useful to you. It is intended to help you understand the life God wants for you, to find that life, and to help others find it as well. I'm writing it because I've been learning to live that life, even as I'm fumbling and stumbling and failing along the way. God has me and some of my closest friends on a remarkable journey together, and I'm hoping others might join us on that journey. Let me start by telling how I got here.

When I heard the gospel as a freshman in college, it made all the sense in the world to me. Jesus came to die on the cross to save me *from* the penalty of my sins and *for* eternal life in heaven someday. I believed it, I accepted it, and I confessed it. And then I went back to my normal, everyday life. I told no one what happened, and no one told me what to do next. Then I started reading the Bible, and I discovered that Jesus and Paul and Peter and James seemed to imply that the Christian life could (or should) look vastly different than it looked before I accepted Christ. They used terms such as *new creature* and *abundant life*, implying that I could (or should) find myself forgiving people, not worrying about things, and loving people that couldn't stand me. They talked about *dying to myself* and *living for Christ*. They implied that I could (or should) stop sinning in some of my tried-and-true ways.

Of course, these ideas sounded good to me. So like a lot of people, I tried to change. I prayed and prayed and prayed. I begged God to change me, to remove life-long sin patterns, to make me new and whole. I tried really hard to be a different person and to do things God's way. And sure enough, I changed a little bit for a little while but inevitably found myself right back where I started. I was floundering. I didn't know the goal of the Christian life, let alone how I should go about getting there. I found out that this whole Christianity thing can be confusing, frustrating, and disappointing. Maybe I was misunderstanding what I was reading, because my life looked very little like the life I read about in the New Testament. Maybe I had failed in some way. Like many people, I began to believe it was not possible.

Maybe you've been there with me. Maybe you're there right now. Many Christians are. Many are struggling to figure out things. Unfortunately, many give up and walk away. Some stay around and hang around the fringes, remaining relatively uninvolved and disengaged.

Others stick around and keep trying. They come to church, serve, give, do Bible studies, join small groups, and go to retreats. But inside they know that these activities haven't made any more difference in their lives than being involved in their local PTA. It's not that these activities are bad. They may be helpful and might even be fun. All in all, the people are nice and the activities are worth the investment of time and money. They just don't seem to make any significant difference. They don't seem to *matter*.

Why is that? Well for me, there were (and oftentimes still are) three main obstacles to change. Maybe you face the same ones.

First, many *don't understand that change is a real possibility*. When asked about the purpose of the Christian life, many of us find ourselves stumped. We just aren't able to articulate where the Christian life is supposed to lead, other than a vague notion of *going to heaven when we die*.

Second, many *don't want to change*. We may *say* we want to change. We may *think* that we want to change. But deep down inside we like things the way they are. After all, we are comfortable with the way things are. We know how the system works. We know that we are OK; it is everyone around us that needs changing. We've learned to accommodate ourselves and the people around us. Plus, changing probably requires some time on our part, and we are busy and probably stretched thin already. Who has time for one more thing?

Finally, even if we truly want to change, most of us *don't know how to change*. Despite our best intentions, we have no idea how to go about it. This book is intended to be a simple guide for allowing God to change us into the kind of people He created us to be. It is not easy and it is not quick...but it is most definitely possible!

The title of this book, *Run in Such a Way*, comes from 1 Corinthians 9:24-27, the first part of God's Word I memorized and meditated on. These verses opened my eyes to the reality that the *Spirit of God* can use the *Word of God* to change the *people of God* into the *image of God*.

> *The Spirit of God can use the Word of God to change the people of God into the image of God.*

I sincerely hope that as you (and maybe some faithful friends) spend time in this book, you will learn how to find the life I am learning to enjoy. May the Holy Spirit come alongside you and enable you to *run in such a way as to get the prize!*

How to Get the Most Out of this Book

I want this book to be as useful as possible to as many people as possible. Toward that end, I'll offer a few suggestions on how to get the most out of it. You may not need the suggestions, but here they are just in case:

1. Some Scripture passages are included in the text of this book, but most are not. It would be best if you took the time to look up each and every one. Perhaps that would be good as you read the book a second time, or as you study out a particular topic in it.

2. Take the opportunity to read this book with a few friends that you think might enjoy it. It is short enough that you might even consider reading the chapter out loud together. Either way, you'll definitely get more out of the book if you read it with someone else. I've included some *Conversation Starters* in Appendix A to help you get going.

3. If you read something that you disagree with or that doesn't make sense, please email me at thomas.houser@gmail.com. I'd love to try to answer your question, and maybe you can answer some of mine!

4. Take notes as you go. Mark things that resonate with you, that you disagree with, or that you've never heard before. Jot down questions you have and discuss them with someone.

1 – The Good News

Living the life God wants for you begins with a better understanding of the Gospel of Jesus Christ. The gospel (or good news) has traditionally referred to the fact that Jesus came to make it possible for people to have their sins forgiven so that they could get into heaven when they die. In order to be *saved* then, a person needs to agree to this arrangement and invite Jesus to be a part of their life. There are many different terms for this, including things like *accepting Christ, praying the sinner's prayer, being baptized for the forgiveness of sins,* or just simply *becoming a Christian.*

This is an absolutely essential part of the gospel that Jesus came to proclaim. It is necessary and good. But it is not the whole gospel. The complete gospel includes the whole story of the Bible, starting with Adam, progressing to the Israelites, and culminating with the birth, life, death, and resurrection of Jesus the Messiah (Acts 13:32-33). Jesus clearly and repeatedly proclaimed this. He came to finish things. He came to complete the story. He was (and is) the good news!

Yes, Jesus came to *save us*. But He also came to *change us*. He came to give us an abundant life (John 10:10; 17:3). He came to make a new life available to anyone who would surrender their kingdom and enter His Kingdom (Luke 9:23-24). He came to usher in the Kingdom of Heaven.

Matthew tells us that throughout His ministry, Jesus preached, "Repent of your sins and turn to God, for the Kingdom of Heaven is near." (Matthew 4:17). He used parables to describe what the Kingdom of Heaven was like (Matthew 5:20; 6:9-10; 13:3-52). He preached the good news of the availability of the Kingdom of God, and He preached it everywhere to the people that were least likely to believe that it was possible. When directly asked by the Pharisees when the Kingdom of Heaven was coming, Jesus told them it was in their midst (Luke 17:20-21).

> *Repent of your sins and turn to God, for the Kingdom of Heaven is near.*

The Kingdom of Heaven can be a complicated thing to understand. The simplest way to think about it is as *the place where God's will is done*. If we embrace this simple understanding, it is clear that His Kingdom is not yet complete. God's final Kingdom will not rule the universe until Christ's return (2 Timothy 4:1-8). Until then, all is not right with the world. We are living in a time when God allows His creatures to defy Him and to rule themselves.

However, it is also clear that through the finished work of Christ and the presence of the Holy Spirit, His Kingdom is already available to rule in the hearts and lives of His followers. His Kingdom *can come* and His will *can be done* in us in increasing measure (Colossians 1:9-14). As He reigns in us, His Kingdom can spread throughout the body of Christ...His church. The church can increasingly be a place where His Kingdom comes and His will is done!

It is this Kingdom Gospel (Matthew 9:35) that asks and answers the four most important questions in the world:

What is really wrong?

> From the very first person, mankind has rebelled against our Creator and King. We are spiritually dead, guilty, and separated from God because of this sin. This separation is complete and it is eternal. Romans 3:23, 6:23a, Ephesians 2:1-3.

What did God do to solve the problem?

> Jesus came, died, and was resurrected so that our sins could be forgiven and so that His kingdom would be available to us. We play no part in this solution; it is totally the work of God. His grace alone is the

foundation of the solution. Matthew 4:17; Ephesians 2:4-8; Romans 6:23b, 5:8; Colossians 1:19-20, 2 Timothy 1:10.

What do we do to take part in the solution?

Believe the gospel and recognize Jesus as our Savior and our Lord. This means surrendering everything in our kingdom in order to live and serve in His Kingdom. Our faith alone is the foundation of our response. Matthew 5:20, 16:24-25; Mark 10:15; John 1:12, 3:5, 10:9; Luke 9:23-24; Romans 10:9.

What happens when we respond?

Peace with God. Adoption as a son or daughter. New life in His Kingdom. Unity in Christ. Forgiveness of sin. Freedom from sinful patterns. Christ in us to change us for His glory. John 10:10; Acts 10:36; Romans 5:1-2, 8:10-12; Colossians 3:10; Philippians 2:13; Galatians 4:4-6.

Most people's understanding of the Gospel includes a lot of clarity around the first two questions, but only a vague understanding of the last two. Oftentimes, "accepting Christ" is thought of as an insurance policy of some kind. I've heard this called the gospel of sin management, in that it is concerned only with how to deal with sin and its effects. In this context, the only thing that matters is the forgiveness of an individual's sin. In other words, the idea of a transformed character and life is not a significant part of this gospel message.

Instead, the main point is securing a place in heaven someday. There isn't much consideration of what to do between now and then. It often includes belief, but not surrender. It often includes accepting God's gift of eternity, without any consideration of becoming the kind of person that would actually enjoy that eternity with him.

But as Oswald Chambers writes, "salvation is not merely deliverance from sin, nor the experience of personal holiness; the salvation of God is deliverance out of self entirely into union with Himself."[1]

A gospel that does not include surrender and an expectation of change "costs abiding peace, a life penetrated throughout by love, faith that sees everything in the light of God's overriding governance for good, hopefulness that stands firm in the most discouraging of circumstances, power to do what is right and withstand the forces of evil. In short, [it] costs you exactly that abundance of life Jesus said he came to bring."[2]

Take for instance two people attending the same church that seem to share the same faith. They both attend church, both read their Bibles, and both affirm the same general beliefs about Christianity. Both say, "I am a Christian." And yet when observed, one of them is most often peaceful, joyful, forgiving, and humble, while the other one is most often anxious, angry, judgmental, and proud. How is this possible? How could two people with the same beliefs be so fundamentally different?

There are many possible explanations for this. We don't like to say it, but it is possible that one is not a Christian at all due to ignorance, misunderstanding, or defiance of the gospel message. One may be completely unaware of the possibility of becoming different. One may intentionally stay the same because he fears what might happen if he changes.

In short, one may simply be a convert while the other is a disciple, as outlined in an article titled "We're Called to Make Disciples, Not Converts" by Tyler Edwards in *Relevant* magazine:

- Converts are believers who live like the world. Disciples are believers who live like Jesus.

- Converts are focused on their values, interests, worries, fears, priorities, and lifestyles. Disciples are focused on Jesus.

- Converts go to church. Disciples are the church.

- Converts cheer from the sidelines. Disciples are in the game.

- Converts hear the word of God. Disciples live it.

- Converts follow the rules. Disciples follow Jesus.

- Converts are all about believing. Disciples are all about being.

- Converts are comfortable. Disciples make sacrifices.

- Converts talk. Disciples make more disciples.[3]

As much as we would like to, we are not in the position to determine who is a convert and who is a disciple. Although we can make a educated guess from observing an individual's life, we cannot know for sure. But I think it is safe to agree with Timothy Keller that one has been "feeding on the Gospel" more deeply than the other:

"You cannot change such things through mere willpower, through learning Biblical principles and trying to carry them out. We can only change permanently as we take the gospel more deeply into our understanding and into our hearts. We must feed on the gospel, as it were, digesting it and making it part of ourselves. That is how we grow."[4]

Whatever the reason, it is very likely that one has been actively training in the Kingdom of God or has been pursuing that life for a longer period of time than the other. Either way, both of them are intended to live a fantastic life alongside Jesus in His Kingdom...but only one is actually doing so.

2 – Vision, Intention, and Means

Living the life God wants for us begins with a better understanding of the Gospel of Jesus Christ. If we understand eternal life to be something that starts when we get to heaven someday, we will miss out on the life He has for us between now and then. And the life God has in mind for us is the most fantastic life we could ever live!

But understanding that this life is possible isn't enough. It won't just automatically happen. We can't just want it and expect it to appear. Trying really hard won't work either. No, we need more. We need what Dallas Willard called *VIM*: vision, intention, and means[5]. We need a compelling *vision* of God and what life with Him would look like. We need the *intention* to pursue that life above everything else. And we need the *means* to pursue it. We need all three or the whole thing won't work. Without a compelling vision and a clear destination, we'll quickly find ourselves discouraged. If we go into it with no clear intention to wholeheartedly pursue it, we'll get distracted and lose interest. And our clearest vision and best intentions will fall short if we don't have the means to pursue it in a meaningful way.

Vision. Intention. Means.

A picture of the destination. The intention to make it there. The means to make the trip.

In this way, living the Christian life is just like any other worthwhile goal. Let's suppose you want to learn to speak Chinese, to be in good physical condition, to cook, or to fly a plane. You won't automatically learn to fly a plane just because you want to. You can't speak Chinese just by mustering up the effort to make the words come out of your mouth. You'll never be a great cook by accident or get in shape by reading magazines about it. If you have a half-hearted vision for learning to fly a plane, you'll never learn to fly. You'll get distracted, run out of money, or simply move on to the next thing.

But what if you had a clear vision of what it would be like to get in shape? You've had a couple of minor health issues: high blood pressure and other stress-related symptoms. You have friends that exercise regularly. You've heard stories of increased energy and better concentration. You'd love to be in better shape so that you can play with your kids. Although you've started working out dozens of times in the past, something really compels you to do it this time.

You can picture yourself jogging with your spouse, playing soccer with your kids, or canoeing down the river. You imagine what it will feel like to fit into your clothes...or even buy new ones because the old ones don't fit!

And so you resolve to do anything necessary to make it happen. Your intention would be clear: You <u>are</u> going to get in shape!

With that clear vision and intention firmly in your mind, you would set out to discover the means to make it happen. After enlisting some help from a qualified trainer, you would begin training. You would start running regularly and intentionally. If you are like me, you'd  have to start eating differently...maybe VERY differently. You'd need more rest, better shoes, and maybe the latest gadget to track your miles, heart rate, etc. You'd learn new exercises, and find the ones that suit you best. You'd even have to adjust your schedule because of the time commitment required to make this happen.

Your vision keeps you encouraged. Your intention keeps you focused. And you weave the means to make it happen into your daily routine...or you change your routine altogether. You save money to get a gym membership. You quit your book club to save time for running. Instead of soda and chips you have water and protein bars. You get up early and hit the gym. Slowly but surely, you see results. Your weight goes down, along with your blood pressure.

Eventually, over time, living that new life is no longer such a struggle, because it is becoming a very real part of you!

Vision

As I mentioned, in some ways, living the Christian life is just like pursuing any other worthwhile goal. However, it is also vastly different. The vision seems less defined, and it's hard to have clear intentions to pursue a fuzzy vision. And the means seem even more confusing. What exactly are we supposed to do?

This whole conversation must start with some clarity around the vision that must permeate the Christian life. This is not a vision of a church building, a church family, or a better life for us. It isn't a vision of freedom from sin or making it to heaven someday. It isn't a vision of health or happiness. Don't misunderstand: These things are just fine, but they have two primary shortcomings.

First, *they are focused on us, not God.* One of the most basic issues with mankind is that everything ends up being about us. We naturally tend to leave God out of the picture. But "God has given [us] the gift of his Son, not to make [our] little kingdom successful, but to welcome [us] to a much better kingdom."[6] God is not interested in satisfying us with physical comforts, easy relationships, or pleasant circumstances. He "wants us to experience hunger so deep that it drives us to forsake these things and finally find our satisfaction in him."[7] We will flourish in remarkable ways as we live lives that reflect Jesus, but if our own flourishing is the primary motivator, we will quickly veer off course in our walk with the Lord.

Second, while these things may move us for a season, *they are not big enough to move us for a lifetime.* We will need to continually cast and catch new visions to re-motivate ourselves. *The only vision that will move us and sustain us for a lifetime is the vision of God Himself and what a life lived with Him would be like.* All this reminds me of a great quote from A.W. Tozer: "What comes into our minds when we think about God is the most important thing about us."[8]

"Think of some of the times in your life when you were greatly moved. Your first feeling of true love, the most beautiful scenery on a beautiful morning, the sweetest smell ever to grace your nose. The warmest glow upon your face, the joy of your child, or immense relaxation following a tough day. Recall that vision and multiply it by infinity. Now you've

*got a tiny taste of what it feels like to be captured
by the vision of God." - Roy.*

Let me try to explain by using a couple of examples from
Scripture that provide a vision of God and show what it
looks like when people find themselves caught up in that
vision. First, here is one from an Old Testament Psalm:

Come, let us sing to the Lord!
Let us shout joyfully to the Rock of our salvation.
Let us come to him with thanksgiving.
Let us sing psalms of praise to him.
For the Lord is a great God, a great King above all gods.
*He holds in his hands the depths of the earth and the
mightiest mountains.*
The sea belongs to him, for he made it.
His hands formed the dry land, too.
Come, let us worship and bow down.
*Let us kneel before the Lord our maker, for he is our
God.*
*We are the people he watches over, the flock under his
care.*
If only you would listen to his voice today! - Psalm 95:1-7

Read it again, slowly. Let the words paint a picture in
your head. Let His Word reveal a vision of God.

This old spiritual song screams out a vision of God
Himself. He is the Rock, the great God, King above all
others. He is immeasurably big, unthinkably powerful,
and timelessly ancient. He made us from nothing, and yet

He saves us and cares for us. He is altogether different than we are and yet invites us to be with Him. This passage also paints a picture of how his people respond to Him as our understanding of Him increases. We shout joyfully, singing loud songs of thanksgiving and praise to Him! We must worship him with our whole being, bowing low in reverence to the King of Kings. We can experience comfort and peace as we listen to His voice and understand His great care for us. It is an amazing and moving vision because it is not in any way a vision of us...it is a vision of Him!

Second, let's look at a reminder to the people in the letter to the Hebrews.

You have not come to a physical mountain, to a place of flaming fire, darkness, gloom, and whirlwind, as the Israelites did at Mount Sinai. For they heard an awesome trumpet blast and a voice so terrible that they begged God to stop speaking. They staggered back under God's command: "If even an animal touches the mountain, it must be stoned to death." Moses himself was so frightened at the sight that he said, "I am terrified and trembling."

No, you have come to Mount Zion, to the city of the living God, the heavenly Jerusalem, and to countless thousands of angels in a joyful gathering. You have come to the assembly of God's firstborn children, whose names are written in heaven. You have come to God himself, who is the judge over all things. You have come to the spirits of the righteous ones in heaven who have now been made perfect. You have come to Jesus, the one who mediates the new covenant between God and people, and to the sprinkled blood, which speaks of forgiveness instead of crying out for vengeance like the blood of Abel. – Hebrews 12:18-24

Again, we see Scripture pointing to the majesty of the living God. Read it again. Close your eyes and picture the scene described in the first few sentences.

Imagine a mountain with flaming fire, overwhelming darkness, and wind as violent as the harshest storm. It would be terrifying, to say the least! But that is not what it is like for us. When we come to God, we see a vision of Him as He is: surrounded by powerful angels, worshipped by the saints of old. We see the One who is perfectly suited to judge all things correctly. But perhaps most beautifully, we see Jesus. In Him, we see that same powerful God as a spotless lamb, our intercessor and savior. We see forgiveness that washes us clean as snow. We see His unthinkably great love for us, and it moves us even more than His indescribable power. We see Him and we celebrate!

Each of us will catch this vision of God in different ways and at different times, but we must catch it.

Each of us will catch this vision of God in different ways and at different times, but *we must catch it*. For me, I first saw it more than ten years after I became a Christian. Yep...ten years! I had been doing the typical church things for some time: attending church services, singing songs, praying, reading the Bible, attending and leading Life Groups, serving in the children's ministry, and volunteering to serve on committees. My family and I even participated in the planting of a new church. My life was going along just fine, and I was perfectly content.

Then I attended a local men's conference with 15,000+ other men. The whole thing was good, but when the music started, I felt a pull on my heart that I had felt before but always pushed away. This time, for whatever reason, I didn't push it away. That evening, the Holy Spirit used the music to carry me away into the presence of the King! I sang at the top of my lungs with my hands in the air. Tears rolled down my face. I saw Him. For the first time ever, my vision expanded past little glimpses into a full-fledged experience with Him. I was never the same. That experience overwhelmed me and changed me. My vision was no longer me, my family, or my church. It was HIM! I saw Him, and from that moment on, He was who I pursued. Even now I stumble, fall, and fail, but what gets me back up is that vision of Him.

Since then, many other experiences and people have renewed and refreshed that vision. Most of them have been much smaller, much quieter, and much simpler. But the vision of God remains embedded and renewed in me. And when it fades, I have learned ways to rekindle it.

That's how I first caught the vision, but everyone is different. God reveals Himself to each of us in different ways and at different times. I can't tell you when or how He will do it. But I can tell you that if you open yourself up to Him you will experience Him...and you will be blown away!

Intention

A clear vision is vital to living life in the Kingdom, but a vision without a clear intention to live it out is impotent. God does not force anything on us, but let's be honest about something. We spend our time doing what is important to us. We cannot be a true follower of Jesus Christ out of a sense of obligation. In order to live in the Kingdom, we have to genuinely *want* to live in it. *If we do not want it first and most, we will not seek it out.*

Maybe that's what Jesus meant in Matthew 6:33 where He said, *"Seek the Kingdom of God above all else, and live righteously, and he will give you everything you need."*

And so, we must figure out what is most important to us. We must figure out what we really want Jesus to do for us (Matthew 20:29-33). We cannot move forward in any meaningful way without knowing where we want to end up.

Author Ruth Haley Barton put it this way:

> *"Jesus' interactions with the people he came in contact with during his life on earth make it clear that desire, and the willingness to name that desire in Christ's presence, is a catalytic element of the spiritual life. It is one of the most powerful motivators for a life lived consistently with intentionality and focus."*[9]

In short, we will never do what we don't set out to do. It really is that simple. In fact, when our intentions are focused on anyone or anything other than Christ, we are actually working against Him.

> *"Anyone who isn't with me opposes me, and anyone who isn't working with me is actually working against me."* –
> *Matthew 12:30*

Means

I believe it is impossible to move forward with intention unless we have a clear vision of God and how fantastic it would be to live life with Him. Finding and fostering that vision is absolutely critical. Though the vision grows and changes as we mature in our faith, we must have some piece of that vision to fuel our race.

But then what? Having a clear vision will get you going in the right direction and you might have the best intentions in the world. But that isn't enough to bring about the realization of that vision. For that, we need more help. We need the means to make progress. We need some instruction. And so we turn to see what the Bible tells us.

There are many places that we could look in Scripture to help us figure out what we are supposed to do. In fact, there are so many places to look that it can sometimes be confusing. But as we spend more and more time in the Bible, some themes start to develop. Let's start with some of Jesus' own words about how to enter and live in His Kingdom.

"Enter through the narrow <u>gate</u>; for the <u>gate</u> is wide and the <u>way</u> is broad that leads to destruction, and there are many who enter through it. For the <u>gate</u> is small and the <u>way</u> is narrow that leads to life, and there are few who find it." - Matthew 7:13-14 (NASB)

Here, Jesus uses an analogy of two gates, two ways, and two destinations. Entering through a *particular gate* opens up an *obvious way* that leads to a *predictable destination*.

First, there is a wide gate that opens up the *broad way*. The broad way of life is spacious, roomy and easy. It is the broad way of 'life as normal.' It's very crowded because it is easy to find and easy to stay on. After all, everything about us and our culture leads us to it and keeps us on it. It seems like the right way to go (Proverbs

14:12). Unfortunately, it leads to destruction, marking out an easy-to-follow route to our own eternal ruin.

But Jesus also says that there is a small gate that opens up the *narrow way*. It is the narrow way of God. There are only a few people on the narrow way, because it is very difficult to find and to stay on. Everything about *us* and our *culture* hides it from us and draws us from the narrow way. And although this way is difficult, it is the only way that leads to life. The narrow way is the only way to the life God intended for us: a life lived alongside the King in the beauty of His Kingdom.

I'll promise you this: We will not drift our way into such a life...we must intentionally pursue it.

"We still have to live in the world, but not as the world does. We need to be a light to those trying to find their way to the narrow gate. The wide road is lit up like Las Vegas. It is easy to follow, but the narrow road is not that attractive and somewhat rough traveling." - Rodger.

So how do we find that small gate and what happens when we walk through it? What does the life look like? And how do we find and stay on the narrow way? Keep reading!

CROSS OF KINGDOM LIVING

3 – The Gate

Grace Point Community Church (the church where I serve) has developed an illustration to help answer these questions. We call it the *Cross of Kingdom Living*. Let's go through it and see if it helps paint a clearer picture.

It all starts by walking through the small gate, surrendering to Christ Himself. In doing this, we understand the depth of our need, rely on the power of God's grace, and commit our lives to Him. As we walk through that gate, He asks us to consider what we really want from Him, just as he did the blind beggar Bartimaeus on the road to Jericho. When Bartimaeus asked Jesus to heal him, Jesus asked him a question:

"What do you want me to do for you?" - Mark 10:51

This seems like a strange question for Jesus to ask. Wasn't Jesus acutely aware of Bartimaeus' needs? Didn't He know what Bartimaeus wanted Him to do? Yes, I believe Jesus knew the answer to the question before He asked it. I think Jesus asked the question so that Bartimaeus would wrestle with the answer. He wanted Bartimaeus to say it out loud. "I want to see!"

So what about us? Are we looking for Him to make us a better husband or wife, mother or father, son or daughter? Do we want Him to heal our diseases or to get us out of debt? Are we looking for Him to serve us, or do we intend to serve Him? Are we asking Him to be a part of our life, or are we accepting the call to be a part of His life? Are we surrendering to Him, or are we asking Him to surrender to us? Often we have "certain expectations of who He should be for us, but we don't think about how we should align our lives with Him."[10] Jesus makes it very clear what it means to be one of his followers: It means dying to ourselves and living for Him.

Then he said to the crowd, "If any of you wants to be my follower, you must turn from your selfish ways, take up your cross daily, and follow me. If you try to hang on to your life, you will lose it. But if you give up your life for my sake, you will save it. And what do you benefit if you gain the whole world but are yourself lost or destroyed?"
– Luke 9:23-25

Christ Himself is the gate, and He invites us to surrender our lives, walking through Him into His kingdom.

"Yes, I am the gate. Those who come in through me will be saved. They will come and go freely and will find good pastures. The thief's purpose is to steal and kill and destroy. My purpose is to give them a rich and satisfying life." – John 10:9-10

Walking through the small gate is something we do at a moment in time. In an instant, we are saved by grace through faith in Christ. We are forever held in God's firm grasp, and He will never let go of us. We pass from death to life. We are new creatures. We do not need to walk through that small gate over and over again.

For he has rescued us from the kingdom of darkness and transferred us into the Kingdom of his dear Son, who purchased our freedom and forgave our sins. – Colossians 1:13-14

But there is another problem we must address.

As we live out our everyday life, we will constantly be tempted to take control of things again. We will be drawn to the idea of serving ourselves instead of serving our King. We tend to forget the joy that comes from the Lord, turning instead to the fleeting happiness that comes from the world. We may find ourselves seeing the people around us as competitors instead of God's beloved children. Our minds drift away from the Holy Spirit and toward ourselves...away from life and peace and toward death (Romans 8:6).

And so it is necessary to surrender ourselves to Jesus on a regular basis. Not because we lose our salvation, but because we *lose our way*. We have forgotten Who we belong to. And so every day, maybe many times a day, we must intentionally take up our cross and surrender to Him. Surrender to the King. Follow His lead. Make Him greater and greater in our lives while we become less and less.

> *Not because we lose our salvation, but because we lose our way.*

Then he said to the crowd, "If any of you wants to be my follower, you must turn from your selfish ways, take up your cross daily, and follow me. If you try to hang on to your life, you will lose it. But if you give up your life for my sake, you will save it." - Luke 9:23-24.

These words from Jesus seem to imply not only a one-time decision but a regular practice of surrendering to Him. In this way, we regularly exchange "the fickle fortunes of living life by sheer whimsy for the more productive and satisfying adventure of being guided by God."[11]

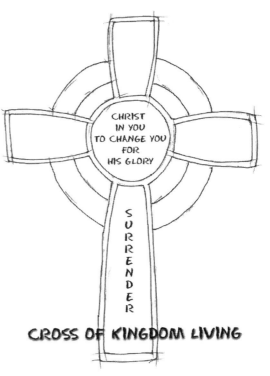

CROSS OF KINGDOM LIVING

4 – The Power and the Purpose

Some amazing things happen when we walk through the small gate of Christ. In an instant, we are adopted into God's family as a full-fledged son or daughter of the King. We are forgiven. We are new creatures. But perhaps the most amazing of all is this: The fullness of God actually lives *in us!* The power of His Son is in us through the presence of the Holy Spirit!

And Christ lives within you, so even though your body will die because of sin, the Spirit gives you life because you have been made right with God. The Spirit of God, who raised Jesus from the dead, lives in you. And just as God raised Christ Jesus from the dead, he will give life to your mortal bodies by this same Spirit living within you. - Romans 8:10-11

This means that we don't have to muster up the power to change ourselves. That's a good thing, because we won't be able to. In fact, we may not really even want to. Thankfully, it is the Holy Spirit that gives us both the desire and the ability to change.

For God is working in you, giving you the desire and the power to do what pleases him. - Philippians 2:13.

It is God who enables us, along with you, to stand firm for Christ. He has commissioned us, and he has identified us as his own by placing the Holy Spirit in our hearts as the first installment that guarantees everything he has promised us. - 1 Corinthians 1:21-22

The Holy Spirit is our counselor and guide. He provides us the power to live the life that we otherwise could not live...or even want to live. He prays on our behalf when we are at a loss for words. He "makes real in [us] the very presence of the Christ. He brings quietness, serenity, strength, and calmness in the face of frustrations and futility."[12] All that the Spirit does in us has a single purpose: to bring God glory! He is in us to change us so that *who we are* will bring glory to God. Christ is in us to change us for His glory!

Now may the God of peace—
who brought up from the dead our Lord Jesus,
the great Shepherd of the sheep,
and ratified an eternal covenant with his blood—

may he equip you with all you need for doing his will.
May he produce in you,
through the power of Jesus Christ,
every good thing that is pleasing to him.
All glory to him forever and ever! Amen. – Hebrews
13:20-21

Paul said it so well: Through His power in us, God intends to produce in us every good thing that is pleasing to Him. And this will bring Him much glory. Francis Chan is right in saying that "when believers live in the power of the Spirit, the evidence in their lives is supernatural. The church cannot help but be different, and the world cannot help but notice."[13]

And the icing on the cake is that the life God has planned for us not only pleases Him and brings Him glory. It also is the best life that we could possibly live. It really is for our good. Christ is in us to change us for His glory and our good. Amen!

> *"Life in the Spirit that is denoted by the term deeper life is far wider and richer than mere victory over sin, however vital that victory may be. It also includes the thought of the indwelling of Christ, acute God-consciousness, rapturous worship, separation from the world, the joyous surrender of everything to God, internal union with the Trinity, the practice of the presence of God, the communion of saints and prayer without ceasing."[14]*

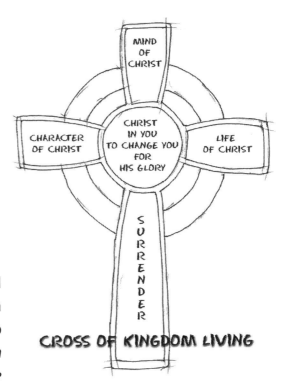

CROSS OF KINGDOM LIVING

5 - The Life

With the power and promise of Christ in us, we are able to experience the *rich and satisfying life* Jesus talked about. The fullness of that life is available to us in an instant, though finding it will take time. That life is intended for God's glory and our good. "The good news as Jesus preached it is not about the minimal entrance requirements for getting into heaven when you die. It is about the glorious redemption of human life—your life."[15]

So what does that life look like? What changes does He intend to make in us? What will we look like when we get there?

When confronted with these questions, many people use the generic term *deep*. For example, they might talk about a *deep* sermon, a *deep* church, a *deep* Bible study, or a *deep* relationship. Author Alan Fadling has this to say about the term *deep*:

> "*My sense of what the average evangelical Christian means by deep is theologically, biblically, doctrinally rich and profound, and this is probably measured mostly in terms of cognitive content. But there are other ways to measure depth.*
>
> *There is soul depth, referring to the dynamics in my life with God and with other people. There is spiritual depth, meaning the level of my personal receptivity to and engagement with God in the moment-to-moment living of life. There is heart depth: I am more emotionally responsive to God and others as well as more willing to show my love for God by obeying him.*
>
> *Are we open to God's bringing such depth to every facet of our lives? Will we enter into deep soul work, deep interaction with God, deep sharing of our lives together and deep engagement with the non-followers in our lives? Will we seek life deep and not settle for just intellect deep?*"[16]

Fadling seems to be echoing Paul's prayers for the church at Philippi, which are both beautiful and instructive:

*I pray that your love will overflow more and more, and that you will keep on growing in **knowledge and understanding**. For I want you to understand what really* *matters, so that you may **live pure and blameless lives** until the day of Christ's return. May you always be filled with the fruit of your salvation—the **righteous character** produced in your life by Jesus Christ—for this will bring much glory and praise to God. - Philippians 1:9-11*

Paul's prayer highlights three of his repeated desires for followers of Christ. First, he wanted them to know and understand more and more of life's spiritual realities. He prayed that their *minds* would be changed. Second, he wanted their character to increasingly reflect the righteous character of Christ Himself. He prayed that their *character* would change. Finally, he wanted their lives to be pure and blameless. He prayed that their *lives* would change. And he reminded them why he wanted these things for them: Such transformation would bring much glory and praise to God!

This is the essence of what it means to grow spiritually: "to live increasingly as Jesus would in our unique place—to perceive what Jesus would perceive if he looked through our eyes, to think what he would think, to feel what he would feel, and therefore to do what he would do."[17]

In the simplest yet most profound way imaginable, **this is the life!** This is the work He intends to do in us. He intends to make us more like His

In the simplest yet most profound way imaginable, this is the life!

Son: to increasingly have the mind of Christ, the character of Christ, and the life of Christ. This is the "rich and satisfying life" Jesus talked about. It is a life of peace and joy. It is a life of contentment. It is a life of trust and obedience. It is a life spent worshipping the King. It is a life that sees people and things as God sees them. It is life where we do the right thing at the right time for the right reason!

Then Jesus said, "Come to me, all of you who are weary and carry heavy burdens, and I will give you rest. Take my yoke upon you. Let me teach you, because I am humble and gentle at heart, and you will find rest for your souls. For my yoke is easy to bear, and the burden I give you is light." – Matthew 11:28-30

Such a life is not easy to find. We will meet fierce resistance from our family and friends, the world around us, and most importantly from ourselves. But the life itself is actually a light burden. We are no longer relying on ourselves, but on Christ. Contentment reigns as we increasingly entrust ourselves to Christ's control and care. Instead of trying to cover over lies with more lies, we find ourselves simply telling the truth. Instead of envying other people's relationships and things, we find ourselves grateful for our own relationships and things. Instead of trying to get ahead of others, we find ourselves trying to help others get ahead. We grow increasingly at peace instead of being full of anger, pride, or lust.

This is the life God most wants for you, and it is the best life you could ever imagine. "We are promised such a life. It has been provided for us and is made possible by the unrelenting effort of Christ on our behalf."[18]

The Mind of Christ

*I pray that your love will overflow more and more, and that you will keep on growing in **knowledge and understanding**. - Philippians 1:9*

One of Jesus' most pervasive themes was one of challenging people to reconsider what they thought to be true. In conversation after conversation, He tried to help people see things from God's perspective instead of their own.

This is particularly easy to see in Matthew chapter 5, where He continually says, "You've heard it said...but I say to you..."

Throughout this portion of Matthew, Jesus challenges the conventional wisdom on things such as murder, adultery, divorce, vows, retaliation, love, hate, good deeds, prayer, and fasting. You think murder is bad? Yes it is, but being angry with someone is just as bad. Do you like to pray? Good, but consider *why* you like to do it in public settings.

He also spends a great deal of time challenging people's perception of God and His Kingdom. Since mankind was first created, we have continually re-imagined who God is and what He is like to suit ourselves. Our families, our culture, and even our churches have taught us to see things from an earthly perspective, not a heavenly one. In Christ, we are told to refocus on the heavenly.

Since you have been raised to new life with Christ, set your sights on the realities of heaven, where Christ sits in the place of honor at God's right hand. Think about the things of heaven, not the things of earth. For you died to this life, and your real life is hidden with Christ in God. – Colossians 3:1-3

Unfortunately, we take these preconceived notions into our life with Christ. Part of our new life with Christ includes unlearning what we think we know about these things and learning to think about them the way that Jesus does. Nearly everything we believe must change, but there are a few things that are particularly important. We need to learn how Jesus would have answered these questions and then come to share His beliefs:

What is the Bible?

What is God like?

Who is God the Father?

Who is Jesus Christ?

Who is the Holy Spirit?

What is mankind?

What is sin?

What is salvation?

What is the church?

What are heaven and hell?

What is spiritual warfare?

What is life in God's Kingdom intended to be like?

There is one significant complication in all this: We aren't always the best judge of what we actually believe. In a 2008 conference at Willow Creek, I heard John Ortberg talk about three different kinds of beliefs:

1. *Public beliefs*: These are things that we *say* we believe that we don't really believe. A less diplomatic way of labeling these beliefs is to simply call them what they are...lies. We lie to get something we want or to avoid something we don't want.

2. *Private beliefs*: These are things that we *think* we believe but our lives reveal that we don't really believe them. For example, we may *think* that we believe the Bible is the inspired, inerrant word to us. But when we choose not to read it or ignore what it says when we do read it, our actual beliefs are revealed. We may *think* that we believe lying is a *terrible* thing to do, but our actions reveal that

we actually believe lying to be very *helpful when we need it.*

3. *Core beliefs*: These are things that we *actually* believe based on the how we live our lives. We don't have to convince ourselves to live a certain way based on these beliefs...we will do it naturally. For example, I don't have to convince myself not to walk off tall buildings, because I believe that gravity will take over and I'll hurt myself.

Jesus was the only person in human history whose public beliefs (what He said He believed), private beliefs (what He thought He believed), and core beliefs (what He actually believed) were in perfect sync. As we receive more and more of the mind of Christ, we will find the same thing to be truer and truer of us!

The Character of Christ

*May you always be filled with the fruit of your salvation—the **righteous character** produced in your life by Jesus Christ—for this will bring much glory and praise to God. - Philippians 1:11*

While the religious leaders of His day seemed most concerned with people's actions, Jesus seemed more concerned with people's motivations. They looked at the outside; Jesus looked at the inside. They judged what they could see of people's lives; Jesus discerned what was true in their hearts.

As we continue to think more and more like Christ, we'll find our character changing as well. Our hearts will be purified. Our motives will be purified. Our character will reflect the world less and less and Christ more and more. Instead of being directed by our flesh, we'll be directed more and more by the Holy Spirit Himself!

Dictionary.com defines character as "the aggregate of features and traits that form the individual nature of a person." Here is Paul's description of the features and traits of our sinful nature (our character):

When you follow the desires of your sinful nature, the results are very clear: sexual immorality, impurity, lustful pleasures, idolatry, sorcery, hostility, quarreling, jealousy, outbursts of anger, selfish ambition, dissension, division, envy, drunkenness, wild parties, and other sins like these. Let me tell you again, as I have before, that anyone living that sort of life will not inherit the Kingdom of God. – Galatians 5:19-21

In contrast, consider his description of the features and traits of our new nature (our character) when we allow the Holy Spirit to change us:

But the Holy Spirit produces this kind of fruit in our lives: love, joy, peace, patience, kindness, goodness, faithfulness, gentleness, and self-control. There is no law against these things! Those who belong to Christ Jesus have nailed the passions and desires of their sinful nature to his cross and crucified them there. – Galatians 5:22-25

Imagine a life characterized by these things! Experiencing true love. Having lasting joy. Enjoying a peaceful attitude. Being supernaturally kind and good and faithful. Being gentle and self-controlled. This is the kind of character God wants to produce in our lives! He wants us to become like Him in this way. He wants our new nature to reflect His nature!

Put on your new nature, and be renewed as you learn to know your Creator and become like him. – Colossians 3:10

The Life of Christ

*For I want you to understand what really matters, so that you may **live pure and blameless lives** until the day of Christ's return. – Philippians 1:10*

Years ago, there was a slogan that became very popular in Christian circles: "What Would Jesus Do?" It was shortened to WWJD, and found its way onto wristbands, bumper stickers, and T-shirts. It was a very effective way to help people consider what Jesus would do in any given situation.

What most people failed to consider was that in order to do what Jesus would do, we need to think the way Jesus thinks and have the character that Jesus has. *Doing*, it turns out, is a by-product of *thinking* and *being*. As we begin to have the mind of Christ and the character of Christ, we'll find ourselves engaging in five different ways of living that are unique to followers of Christ:

1. *Belonging* to one another: Developing deeper relationships, treating people differently, and practicing reconciliation.

2. *Growing* in spiritual maturity: Discipling others, living a generous life (both materially and spiritually), and recognizing and battling spiritual opposition in our life.

3. *Serving* our church family through our unique spiritual gifts, passions, abilities, personality, and experiences.

4. *Sharing* our faith with a lost world with actions and words. As the Holy Spirit spreads "the love of God in our hearts, we begin deliberately to identify ourselves with Jesus Christ's interests in other people."[19]

5. *Worshipping* God with every part of our lives.

Jesus lived in a way that perfectly reflected His beliefs and His character. He created a deep community with His disciples and their extended circles. He grew in stature and wisdom and lived a life intent on helping mature the faith of others. He served as He was called to serve and taught others to do the same. He shared the essence of true faith with everyone with whom He came in contact. And He certainly loved His Father and worshipped in obedience to Him at all times.

Jesus also wants us to live lives that are productive in His Kingdom. In John 15:5, Jesus says, *"Yes, I am the vine; you are the branches. Those who remain in me, and I in them, will produce much fruit. For apart from me you can do nothing."*

"This is not only possible but certain if the branch remains in union with the vine. Uniformity of quantity and quality are not promised. But if the life of Christ permeates a disciple, fruit will be inevitable."[20]

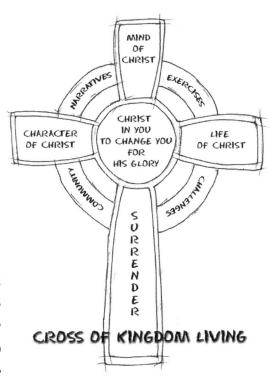

CROSS OF KINGDOM LIVING

6 – The Way

We've come a long way around the Cross of Kingdom Living. We surrender ourselves to the King, and He takes us from death to life. We catch the vision of the Christian life, and it makes more and more sense to us. We have the power and purpose of God living in us. He even gives us a wholehearted intention to pursue that life. We see it! We want it!

Now we just have to figure out the way to find that life. The apostle Paul found himself in a similar place in his ministry.

Do you not know that in a race all the runners run, but only one gets the prize? Run in such a way as to get the prize. Everyone who competes in the games goes into strict training. They do it to get a crown that will not last, but we do it to get a crown that will last forever. Therefore I do not run like someone running aimlessly; I do not fight like a boxer beating the air. No, I strike a blow to my body and make it my slave so that after I have preached to others, I myself will not be disqualified for the prize. – 1 Corinthians 9:24-27 (NIV)

Paul had been captured by a vision of winning his race with the Lord. He intended to do what was necessary to win it...and then he actually did it. He went into "strict training" so that he could stay in the race. This training included getting the counsel of Jesus' disciples, prayer, suffering, and re-thinking his religious background in light of the gospel of Jesus Christ. He worked very hard to finish his race well. It was not easy, but it was necessary.

I believe that Paul's physical training analogy was perfect. Although I've worked out sporadically in the past, in late 2014 I caught a vision of a life lived in a body that was in better condition. I pictured running around the yard with grandkids (although they are many years away...I hope). I pictured long hikes with my wife Michele. Most of all, I pictured the increased energy and healthier mind that comes along with a healthier body.

So this time, I did things differently. I found a couple good friends with whom to work out. They encouraged me to show up to the gym when I really didn't want to go. I enrolled in a 12-week "fitness challenge" where I learned to eat better and more intentionally.

I also hired a personal trainer for a short time. Although Damian Buck nearly killed me, he showed me that it was actually possible to work out hard and get better at it! He challenged me and encouraged me all at the same time. (By the way, the dude pictured here is not me...it is Damian.)

In short, I began to learn and practice the *way* of physical fitness and healthier eating. My vision and intention would have been of no use without learning and practicing the steps necessary to make it happen. I've started out well, and I want to continue to work very hard to finish this physical race well. It was not easy, but it was necessary.

It is necessary in the spiritual realm as well. The natural momentum of this world is away from Christ and His Kingdom. After years of living in the world, the natural momentum of our minds, character, and lives is the same. Our hearts and minds and bodies have grown accustomed to our old way of thinking, acting, and interacting with the world. Our background, our education, our families, and even our workplaces teach us to live in ways that are contrary to God's design. In essence, our *new lives* don't fit with our *old selves*. We just aren't well-suited to live this new life. So for us to experience that new life, we must walk the narrow way of Christ. We have to *make every effort* to respond to His grace in us (2 Peter 1:5-9). We have to *do something*. God saves us and works in us, but God will not give us good habits or good character...we have to *do something!* He invites us to take an active role in our own transformation. He invites us to *do something.*

We have to do something!

Don't misunderstand me here. We are saved by *grace alone* through *faith alone*. Our effort cannot earn God's favor or increase His love for us. Any effort we make must be done on the foundation of our faith in response to God's grace.

God saved you by his grace when you believed. And you can't take credit for this; it is a gift from God. Salvation is not a reward for the good things we have done, so none of us can boast about it. – Ephesians 2:8-9

But even mentioning the need for effort makes some people quite nervous. To them, any suggestion that we play a role in our own spiritual maturity is a suggestion that we are failing to rely on God's grace in our lives. If this is difficult for you, consider this thought from Dallas Willard:

"We find it hard to see that grace is not opposed to effort, but is opposed to earning. Earning and effort are not the same thing. Earning is an attitude, and grace is definitely opposed to that. But it is not opposed to effort. When you see a person who has been caught on fire by grace, you are apt to see some of the most astonishing efforts you can imagine."[21]

Willard seems to be echoing the Apostle Paul's thoughts on this. In his first letter to the church at Corinth, we read about God's *supernatural ability* to make Paul's *human effort* effective in changing him from being Christianity's greatest persecutor to being its greatest instructor:

But whatever I am now, it is all because God poured out his special favor on me—and not without results. For I have worked harder than any of the other apostles; yet it was not I but God who was working through me by his grace. - 1 Corinthians 15:10

If you recall, Christ described His "narrow way" as narrow because it is filled with difficulty and struggle. It is the narrow way of God, not the broad way of humanity. There are only a few people on it, because it is very difficult to find and to stay on. Everything about us and our culture hides it from us and draws us from it. But it is also the way that leads to life. Jesus' way is the only way to experience the rich and satisfying life He promises.

"It amuses me that society conditions us to want to make things 'easy'. Muscles are never formed from 'easy'...spiritual or physical." - Penny.

There are countless ways to describe the narrow way of Christ. Understanding this, Grace Point's elders prayerfully searched the Scriptures, consulted ancient and modern experts, and recalled our own personal experiences. All of that work helped us narrow down the countless ways to four general categories. We believe these four categories contain the main ways of Christ. We believe they are the primary ways that God works in us to change us for His glory.

The four include:

1. *Learning new narratives*: learning to perceive life the way Jesus did instead of the way we have grown to do.

2. *Practicing soul exercises*: training alongside the Holy Spirit in order for Him to retrain our minds, hearts, and bodies.

3. *Living in community*: being with like-minded people that will encourage and challenge us.

4. *Experiencing life challenges*: allowing God to use the difficult experiences in life to shape us.

In short, we will not change just because we *want* to change. We will not change just because we *try* to change. We will change only if and when we *train* to change. Even though we have been granted a new life in Christ, the thoughts and desires of our old life still remain in us. We have to change how we think (our narratives), how we practice (the soul exercises), who we interact with (our community), and how we respond to difficulty (our life challenges). If we come alongside the Holy Spirit and allow Him to work in us, true life change will come more naturally to us.

Learning New Narratives

A great deal of our understanding about life comes in the form of stories or narratives. We often don't remember the details of any given situation, but if the situation is memorable enough, we'll remember the general narrative of it. We'll remember who was there and what it felt like. Some narratives have certain takeaways that we combine together to form larger narratives in our minds.

James Bryan Smith describes the different kinds of narratives that are likely to shape us as we live our lives:

> "Family narratives are the stories we learn from our immediate families. Our parents impart to us their worldview and their ethical system through stories. Key questions such as Who am I? Why am I here? Am I valuable? Are answered early on in the form of narrative. There are cultural narratives that we learn from growing up in a particular region

57

of the world. From our culture we learn values (what is important, who is successful) in the form of stories and images. Americans, for example, are taught the value of 'rugged individualism' through the stories of our past (the Revolution, the pioneers). There are religious narratives—stories we hear from the pulpit, the classroom and religious books that help us understand who God is, what God wants of us and how we ought to live."[22]

All of these narratives combine in our minds to form one complex, interrelated narrative. Some would call it a worldview. This narrative is the lens through which we perceive the world around us and even how we perceive ourselves. In all of us, this narrative is a mixture of truth, error, illusion, and reality. But at its core, our default narrative provides us with a worldly perspective, not a godly one. Our minds have been trained to perceive and interpret the world around us in a way that is inconsistent with the way of God. It is this reality that ignited Paul to challenge the Christians in Rome.

Don't copy the behavior and customs of this world, but let God transform you into a new person by changing the way you think. Then you will learn to know God's will for you, which is good and pleasing and perfect. - Romans 12:2

"Changing the way you think." This is another way of saying "learn new narratives." In his classic work *My Utmost for His Highest*, Oswald Chambers puts it this way: "No one is ever united with Jesus Christ until he is willing to relinquish not sin only, but his whole way of looking at things."[23]

In particular, we are called to learn Jesus' narratives...the narratives of God's Kingdom. "The kingdom narratives oppose the world's narratives: You are valuable to God. God loves you no matter what. Your worth is not dependent on your performance or on what others think of you. Your worth is found in the loving eyes of God. If you win, God loves you. If you lose, God loves you. If you fast and pray and give your money to the poor, God loves you. If you are sinful and selfish, God loves you. He is a covenant God, and his love never changes. You are valuable, precious and worth dying for just as you are."[24]

Jesus' way of perceiving the world is completely different than the way we are trained to perceive it. We have to take the time to soak ourselves in His true narratives in order to wash away our false ones.

"I recently read through a small book called "The Knowledge of the Holy" by A.W. Tozer. I think that book was a great study of what the character of God is really like. That book really gave me a much deeper understanding of God's fixed and unchanging character and of how these characteristics are at the pinnacle of their power to exist. God is unlimited in anything that is Him, is in Him, that is outside Him! We sin the sins of deserved death, yet

> *He has the power to forgive us even though His character cannot tolerate sin. How awesome is He!"*
> *- Rodger*

New narratives are best learned as we practice soul exercises, live in community with other believers, and experience life challenges. When we are intentionally focused on learning new narratives, we'll find lessons in almost any situation!

Practicing Soul Exercises

Imagine...

- Trying to run a marathon after living life as a couch-potato for the past ten years.

- Trying to play on an MLS soccer team when you've never even seen a soccer ball.

- Trying to navigate the highways around Dallas the first time you try to drive a car.

None of these examples would go well, and we wouldn't expect them to go well. It would be foolish to expect success from even the most valiant effort. These are things we might be able to do well, but not by simply *trying hard*: We would need to *train hard*. There is a vast difference between the two, and it is a difference we must understand.

This same principle is critical in our understanding of how soul exercises fit into the narrow way of Christ. Training hard is difficult, but not as difficult as trying hard. And training hard actually works!

John Ortberg describes it this way:

> *"Respecting the distinction between training and merely trying is the key to transformation in every aspect of life. People sometimes think that learning how to play Bach at the keyboard by spending years practicing scales and chord progressions is the "hard" way. The truth is the other way around. Spending years practicing scales is the easy way to learn to play Bach. Imagine sitting down at a grand piano in front of a packed concert hall and having never practiced a moment in your life. That's the hard way."* [25]

So what is a *soul exercise*? Simply put, a soul exercise "is any practice that enables a person to do through training what he or she is not able to do simply by trying. They are practices, relationships and experiences that bring our minds and bodies into cooperation with God's work in our lives, making us more capable of receiving more of his life and power." [26] Soul exercises have traditionally been known as spiritual disciplines, but the term soul exercise seems to better describe their focus (the soul) and what they are (exercises).

Physical training is good, but training for godliness is much better, promising benefits in this life and in the life to come. – 1 Timothy 4:7-8

It is likely that you are already practicing some soul exercises. Attending worship services, giving, and serving are common ways that Christians train their souls in the way of Christ. Jesus modeled a great many others as well. In fact, "Jesus directed and led his disciples into disciplines for the spiritual life: fasting, prayer, solitude, silence, service, study, fellowship, and so forth."[27]

"I have been fairly consistent for several years in having a daily quiet time, but even this can become just an intellectual activity or something to check off my to-do list. One thing that has helped me go deeper in my times with God is to journal. I will write out a verse and take it apart word by word, reflecting on how to apply it to my life. Or I will write out a prayer asking God to use me that day and make me aware of His presence. This has transformed my devotional time into a life changing relationship." – Kelly.

How do we know which soul exercises to practice? Now that is a good question! In a lot of ways, we have to approach it backwards. First, we need a good understanding of what it means to really live in the Kingdom of God. Next, we carefully consider what barriers keep us from living that kind of life. Finally, we learn the soul exercises that can help us overcome those barriers.

There are some resources listed in Appendix C of this book that will help you find the right soul exercises for you. But for right now, just keep reading!

Living in Community

Football players do not train in isolation. They work out, practice plays, sweat and bleed together hour after hour, day after day. The team actually makes the individual players better. When it's time to play the game, they are all on the same page working with each other and for each other.

In a similar way, the Christian life was never intended to be lived in isolation. It would certainly be easier and more comfortable to do so, but there are simply too many lessons that can be learned only in the company of other people. Only if you are part of a community of believers seeking to resemble, serve, and love Jesus will you ever get to know Him and grow into His likeness[28].

> *"Trying to live the Christian life without other God-people is like a flame without air: The fire is quickly extinguished." - Reed.*

And as we practice loving one another in community, we are acting as a testimony to a watching world:

"So now I am giving you a new commandment: Love each other. Just as I have loved you, you should love each other. Your love for one another will prove to the world that you are my disciples." - John 13:34-35

As we live in community together, we can motivate and encourage one another:

<u>Let us</u> hold tightly without wavering to the hope we affirm, for God can be trusted to keep his promise. <u>Let us</u> think of ways to motivate one another to acts of love and good works. And <u>let us</u> not neglect our meeting together, as some people do, but encourage one another, especially now that the day of his return is drawing near. - Hebrews 10:23-25.

As painful as it can sometimes be, living in community is the perfect context in which to warn each other, to take care of each other, and to show patience with each other.

Brothers and sisters, we urge you to warn those who are lazy. Encourage those who are timid. Take tender care of those who are weak. Be patient with everyone. - 1 Thessalonians 5:14

> "I have gotten so much out of listening to others in our Life Group meetings and hearing the wisdom that the Lord has imparted to them. Attending the Men's Retreats here and at my other church also brought me closer to the Lord and my brothers in Christ. You learn how to pray better, you learn how to be at ease with others, and you learn how to listen to the Lord." - Rodger

Though many soul exercises are done alone, many of them are best practiced with other Christians. In many cases they are "things Christian people do together over time in response to and in the light of God's active presence."[29] In this way, we can see and hear how the exercises have encouraged and strengthened others. This in turn, will encourage and strengthen us and deepen our faith. "The Christian life is meant to be lived in community, with people who are intentionally with you, who support you and will do what they can to help nurture your faith."[30]

Experiencing Life Challenges

> "If you ask people who don't believe in God why they don't, the number one reason will be suffering. If you ask people who believe in God

> *when they grew most spiritually, the number one answer will be suffering.* "[31]

Perhaps one of the most painful but most fruitful ways the Lord matures us is through the refining fire of life's challenges. We understandably do not seek them out, but He will seek to refine us when we walk through them.

When facing a daunting situation, I often hear people say things like, "Well, the Lord must be doing this for a reason!" That might be true, but we cannot necessarily say that the Lord causes the challenges in our lives. We cause many of our own troubles, and merely living in a broken world guarantees our fair share of them.

> *"For centuries humanity has used God's glorious creation in ways in which God never intended, resulting in many unintended consequences... including cancer. I do not believe God created cancer, and I believe that it grieves him to see his creation experiencing such a dreadful disease. Humanity's sinful ways result in all sorts of consequences, yet God does not leave us to fight alone. He reminds us that as long as we dwell in HIS Kingdom he will fight alongside us. And we have the assurance that He will work through our trials for the good of his people." - Jay*

Regardless of the source, we have the choice to walk into life's challenges with the Lord or without Him. We have the choice to trust Him in the struggle or to walk away from Him. We have the choice to walk through difficulties with a community of friends or to go it alone, forsaking community and its healing presence.

Dear brothers and sisters, when troubles of any kind come your way, consider it an opportunity for great joy. For you know that when your faith is tested, your endurance has a chance to grow. So let it grow, for when your endurance is fully developed, you will be perfect and complete, needing nothing. – James 1:2-4

We can rejoice, too, when we run into problems and trials, for we know that they help us develop endurance. And endurance develops strength of character, and character strengthens our confident hope of salvation. – Romans 5:3-4

Until we are called home to live in God's perfect Kingdom, we will experience challenges. One of the most profound things we can learn is to allow Him to use those challenges to draw us close to Him as He forms us more and more into the image of Christ:

And we know that God causes everything to work together for the good of those who love God and are called according to his purpose for them. For God knew his people in advance, and he chose them to become like his Son, so that his Son would be the firstborn among many brothers and sisters. – Romans 8:28-29

7 – Next Steps

In 2013, my wife and I heard Dallas Willard say something at a conference in Santa Barbara that greatly impacted us both. I think it might impact you as well:

> *"We all live by default or design, but to drift is disaster."*

Our *default* way of living is what we have called the *broad* way. This way is easy to find and easy to stay on. You don't have to look for this life. It will draw you in and lead you to a life lived apart from God. It will lead you to death. In contrast, God's *design* for our life is what we have called the *narrow* way. It is hard to find and hard to stay on. You'll have to go looking for this life. It will not find you, but it can save you!

With that, let me carefully rephrase Dallas' original quote:

We all live by the world's default or the Lord's design. But know this: no one ever drifts accidently to the Lord's design.

In order to live by the Lord's design we need VIM, as discussed in chapter 2. We need a compelling *vision* of God and what life with Him would look like. We need the *intention* to pursue that life above everything else. And we need the *means* to pursue it. We need all three or the whole thing won't work.

Vision. Intention. Means. We have to see the life. We have to want the life. We have to pursue the life. Here are a few things to keep in mind as you consider living the life God designed you to live.

Be Committed

You'll have to be fully *committed* to find the life.

Christianity makes a terrible hobby, so if you intend to pursue it in that way, you probably shouldn't bother. But if you pursue Him before and above everything else, you will find Him!

This goes back to chapter 3 and Jesus' question to the blind beggar named Bartimaeus: "What do you want Me to do for you?" Each of us must ask ourselves some questions here:

What do I want Jesus to do for me?

What are my intentions with Him?

Am I looking for Him to make me a better _____?

Do I hope He'll help me stop _____?

Am I looking for Him to give me a ticket to heaven when I die?

Or...

Do I intend to follow Him and His ways wherever He takes me?

Do I intend to surrender my way of thinking, acting, and interacting to Him?

Do I intend to make Him my master as well as my friend?

Do I intend to do what it takes to become more and more like Him?

Do I intend to make Him the most important person in my life?

These are critical questions to wrestle with, and it is best to be honest with yourself, with God, and with a few other close friends you can trust.

Be Different

You'll have to do something *different* to find the life.

Doing the same things you've always done probably won't work very well. "The direction you are currently traveling—relationally, financially, spiritually, and the list goes on and on—will determine where you end up in each of those respective arenas. This is true regardless of your goals, your dreams, your wishes, or your wants."[32] However, if you're willing to try some new things, you'll soon find new things happening to you.

One of the hardest things for each person to figure out is what their particular *different* looks like. Each of us responds to God and the world around us differently. This means that the "particular combination of practices, relationships, and experiences needed for growth will be different for everyone. We need the freedom to discover how God wants us to grow, for his design will not look quite the same for everyone. Perhaps God speaks to us in special ways through nature. Perhaps he made us to be formed by music. We may have an above-average capacity for silence and prayer. Or we might respond most strongly to images, symbols, and the fine arts."[33] This will probably take some experimentation on your part. It will also be done best in the company of others who are also training in the ways of Jesus.

Having said that, let me introduce you to yet another quote from Dallas Willard. When asked what he would recommend to someone that wants to follow Jesus more closely, Dallas said this:

"Do the next thing that seems right to you."

I know it doesn't seem like much, but I think he was trying to remind us that if we have the Holy Spirit living in us, we should assume that He is already giving us hints as to what to do next. And the reality is that His hints might not fall into a tidy list somewhere. Have you been feeling a nudge to _____? Ask a trusted friend or pastor, check the Word of God...then do it!

If you have trouble coming up with what to do, here are a few suggestions that have worked for millions of people over thousands of years:

- *Pray.* Ask the Holy Spirit to guide you on His way.

- *Read.* Read the Bible (see Hebrews 4:12) as often as you can. The gospels in particular will soak you in the words of Jesus. You might consider reading all the passages listed in Appendix B, which includes every New Testament reference to the Kingdom of God.

- *Go.* Go to church...every week. Make a decision to find and stick with a church family. Introduce yourself to the pastor and take him to lunch. Tell him about your desire to grow, and find out how he can help you.

- *Get involved.* Don't just go to church, get involved at church. If there are Bible studies, join one. If there is a volleyball league, join it. If they need help setting up chairs or playing in the band, help.

- *Get help.* You are almost sure to wander off the narrow way if you don't get some help. Inexperienced marathon runners always find a pace-setter that they can follow. For example, if your goal is to finish in 4 hours 15 minutes, you'd find and follow the appropriate pace-setter. The same is true of the Christian race: Find someone that you can follow "as they follow Christ" (1 Corinthians 11:1).

One more thing. If you are committed to running in such a way as to get the prize, you'll have to adjust your schedule accordingly. "One way you can start seeking God's Kingdom first is by redrafting your schedule and filling it up the way God would fill it if He were in charge of your time, your schedule, your calendar."[34]

More than likely, this will include not only adding some activities but removing some as well. When we have too many things to do, we typically spend less time on relationships, soul exercises, and taking care of ourselves. I would suggest you add one thing and remove two things...even if they are good things. Start small and build from there.

Be Patient

You'll have to be *patient* as you find the life.

Christlikeness doesn't happen overnight. You'll stumble and fall as often as you run and win. But if you give it time, you'll see Christ forming in you more each day! There is no 30-day plan or 12-step method for training in the Kingdom. We take years or decades to develop our narratives, character traits, and physical habits. Though you will experience some breakthroughs, you should expect to take just as long to develop new narratives, new character traits, and new physical habits.

> *"I had first discovered early in my spiritual life that the Lord was drawing me to Himself to understand Him more. I started reading the Bible by reading the New Testament first, then going back and reading the Old Testament. At the end of the Old, I continued right on into the New again and re-read it. I have always encouraged others to read it that way. I have read through the Bible several times. Each time the Lord gave me new insight and understanding to passages I had read before but never grasped." - Rodger.*

Be patient with yourself. It is OK to be *discontent* with your progress, but don't let yourself become *discouraged* by it. Give yourself some time. Don't be in a hurry...

"An unhurried vision of growth and maturity brings freedom and encouragement because we have a whole lifetime to grow. I don't have to keep living the same year of my Christian life over and over again with little actual personal transformation. I am invited into a renewing and deepening awareness of God's love as well as new ways of expressing that love in my ministry to others. I don't have to be the same person spiritually in five years that I am today. My roots can slowly and surely sink deeper into all that God has for me. New branches will grow, branches that were never there before, because old branches have been pruned away. I can trust that God intends my life to be more fruitful than I can imagine."[35]

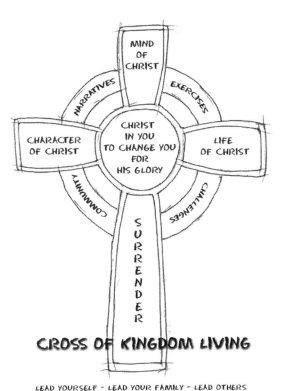

CROSS OF KINGDOM LIVING

LEAD YOURSELF ~ LEAD YOUR FAMILY ~ LEAD OTHERS

8 – One Last Thing

I have to mention just one more thing. Without this last concept, the narrow way of Christ would have died within a few years of Jesus' death and resurrection.

It is simple, but it is important: *This life isn't just for you.*

Life in the Kingdom of God is the best life you could ever live...but it isn't just for you. If you are truly growing in the narrow way of Christ, you will find yourself seeking to lead others into that life as well. As your vision of God and life lived with Him gets clearer, you will most certainly desire for others to see it too. In fact, sharing your new life in the Kingdom was one of Jesus' final commands to his followers:

Jesus came and told his disciples, "I have been given all authority in heaven and on earth. Therefore, go and make disciples of all the nations, baptizing them in the name of the Father and the Son and the Holy Spirit. Teach these new disciples to obey all the commands I have given you. And be sure of this: I am with you always, even to the end of the age." - Matthew 28:18-20.

We aren't told to go alone, but we are told to go. We aren't told to go and make church attendees; we are told to make disciples. We aren't told to dunk people underwater while we repeat the names of Trinity; we are told to immerse them in the reality of life in that Trinity. We aren't told to keep these things to ourselves; we are told to teach others how to live the life.

You have heard me teach things that have been confirmed by many reliable witnesses. Now teach these truths to other trustworthy people who will be able to pass them on to others. - 2 Timothy 2:2

Now, a word of warning on this. When you begin to experience this new life, you will become energized by it. You will be excited by what you see. You will want to share it with others, especially your family and closest friends. This is when training in the Kingdom will get the hardest of all. The reality is that not everyone wants this kind of life. In fact, many people do not want this kind of life. Most people are quite satisfied with the little bit of Jesus they have already but are quite uncomfortable considering giving Him their whole lives.

Here is another word of warning. It may seem obvious to you, but it is a constant struggle for me: You can't make someone want this life. You can't force them to see the vision of God and what a life lived with Him could look like. You can't force them to want it more than anything else. To quote Dallas Willard once again, "You can't push people into the Kingdom. You have to pull them in." You have to let your life speak for itself. You have to seek the Kingdom yourself and continue to invite them to taste it with you. You have to be patient and let their faith be their faith...it isn't yours.

But there is reason for celebration, because *it will happen*. Not with everyone, but with some. They will get a glimpse of it. They will taste it. They will wonder how to get another taste. And they may ask you what they should do.

Be ready for it.

Be ready to say, "Come follow me as I follow Christ!"

Be ready to help them *run in such a way as to get the prize!*

Appendix A - Conversation Starters

This book is short enough to read in an hour. However, my hope is that it is compelling enough to make you think and pray about what it says. This could take many hours.

For those reading this book with a group of friends, I've included some questions for each chapter to help get some good conversations going. I've also included some soul exercises to help you wrestle with your content in each chapter.

Introduction

1. Which of the questions on pages 1 and 2 do you wrestle with the most? Explain why that question is so compelling to you.

2. I shared the struggle to understand my own Christian faith. I wasn't sure what I was supposed to be doing or where I was supposed to be going. What about you? Is the Christian life all you thought it would be? Do you

have a clear understanding of the life God wants for you? Do you know how to get there?

3. I described three main obstacles to change. Which of them resonate with you? Have you faced any obstacles that I didn't mention?

4. Soul Exercise: Write an honest letter to God that explains where you are in your faith, where you'd like to be, and what you think might be holding you back.

1 - The Good News

1. How would you describe the Kingdom of God?

2. How have you traditionally understood the gospel? How does this chapter explain the gospel? What differences, if any, do you see between the two?

3. If you haven't accepted Christ, what is holding you back? What questions do you have? What reservations do you have?

4. Do you count on Christ as both your Savior and your Lord? Do you understand the difference between the two? Explain if/how your day-to-day life backs up your answer.

5. Soul Exercise: Use Appendix B to read through all the references to the Kingdom of God in the four Gospels and jot down how each of them helps complete a picture of the Kingdom.

2 - Vision, Intention, and Means

1. How would you describe the way the three parts of *VIM* (vision, intention, and means) fit together and feed off one another?

2. What is the vision that drives your everyday life and focuses your life's energies and intentions? How was it formed in you? How significant a role does God play in that vision?

3. Spend some time considering this statement: "if our own flourishing is the primary motivator, we will quickly veer off course in our walk with the Lord." Do you agree or disagree? How have you seen it play out in your life or the life of people around you?

4. What are your intentions in life? What drives your day-to-day decisions?

5. Do you think you are on the narrow way or the broad way of life? What about some of the other people you know? Explain if/how day-to-day life backs up your answer.

6. Soul Exercise: Take some time to slowly read the passages from Psalm 95 or Romans 12 in the chapter. Even better, find an audio version of the passage and listen to it several times. Consider the vision of God contained in the passage? Is that a vision large enough to move you and sustain you for a lifetime? Take some time to pray for a larger, more awe-inspiring vision of God and a life lived with Him.

3 - The Gate

1. Have you surrendered to Christ as your Savior and Leader? Explain if/how your day-to-day life backs up your answer.

2. As the chapter discussed, surrendering to Christ is both a one-time event and an on-going need. What areas of life do you struggle to surrender to Him on a regular basis?

3. What do you want more than anything else in the world? What do you really want Jesus to do for you?

4. Here are some questions to help clarify your answers the last question:

   a. What do you worry or complain about the most? What does that reveal about your greatest desire in life?

   b. What are your dreams for the future? What do they reveal about your greatest desire in life?

   c. Based on your Facebook updates, text messages, and casual conversations, what would your friends assume to be your greatest desire in life?

5. Soul Exercise: Read the story of Jesus and Bartimaeus in Mark 10:46-52. Imagine yourself in the story as Jesus. What would you have been thinking, seeing, feeling, wanting? Now, read through the same story from the perspective of the crowd and finally from the perspective of Bartimaeus. Why do you think Jesus asked Bartimaeus the question? What do you think

Bartimaeus' answer revealed about his desires? Where do you find yourself in the story?

4 - The Power and the Purpose

1. How have you traditionally understood God's purpose in and for your life?

2. What is one area of your life you think God wants to transform? Do you think it is possible? Do you think it is probable?

3. How significant is the Holy Spirit in your daily Christian life?

4. Soul Exercise: Look up and consider what the following verses say about the Holy Spirit and the role He intends to play in the life of a Christ-follower. Then, choose one verse to memorize and mediate on for the week. Acts 1:4-8; Acts 2:1-13; Acts 4:31; Romans 8:1-17; Romans 8:26-27; Romans 15:13; 1 Corinthians 2:10-14; 1 Corinthians 3:16; 1 Corinthians 6:9-11; 1 Corinthians 12:1-11; 2 Corinthians 3:17-18; Galatians 4:4-7; Galatians 5:16-25; Galatians 6:6-10; Ephesians 3:14-16; Ephesians 4:21-24; 1 John 4:13.

5 - The Life

1. What questions do you have about the life God intends for you?

2. Do you believe such a life is possible for an ordinary human being? Do you believe it is possible for you?

3. Have you experienced periods of your life that reflect the description on pages 41 and 42? If so, what was it like? If not, why do you think that is?

4. What are some ways that you think differently than Jesus? You might look through the Sermon on the Mount in Matthew 5-7 for some ideas.

5. What are some areas in which your character shows itself to be like that of Galatians 5:19-21?

6. Do you find yourself naturally doing the right thing at the right time for the right motives? What is one area of life that you think God would like to change?

7. Soul Exercise: Go to your local coffee shop, McDonalds, or church foyer and re-read this chapter. After you are done, pray for eyes to see the people around you from God's perspective. Then take some time to observe the people in the coffee shop with these questions in mind:

   a. What would Jesus be thinking as He looked around the same space? How does that compare with what you see as you look around?

   b. Consider how Jesus' character (Galatians 5:19-21) would impact His passions for the people at the coffee shop? How do they compare with your passions?

   c. What would Jesus do if He were sitting in that coffee shop with you right now? How would He respond to what he saw? How could you respond? Will you respond?

6 - The Way

1. Does the idea that spiritual maturity requires effort on our part make you nervous or does it free you to pursue it?

2. What are the dangers inherent in the idea of you needing to work out your faith?

3. What is one thing you have changed your mind about in the recent past? What made you change your mind?

4. Describe a time when you trained for something in particular. Who prescribed the training? Did it help?

5. What soul exercises have you practiced in the past? Which ones have been particularly helpful to you, and why?

6. Describe one positive and one negative experience from being in community with others. What made the positive one so positive? What role did you play in the outcome? What made the negative one so negative? What role did you play in the outcome?

7. Think back to a difficult experience that happened more than a few years ago. What did you learn from it? Is there any other way you could have really learned that lesson?

8. Soul Exercise: Call or write a letter to someone that is (or was) a part of your Christian community, thanking them for walking with you in your faith.

7 - Next Steps

1. Which of the next steps will you find to be the most challenging: being committed, being different, or being patient?

2. Why do you think that is so challenging? What can you do to step up to the challenge?

3. Who do you know that would be a good 'pace-setter' for your Christian race? Why do you think he or she would be valuable?

4. Soul Exercise: Contact the "pace-setter" and set up a time to talk about forming a discipling relationship with them.

8 - One Last Thing

1. Who can you walk with on his or her journey in the Kingdom?

2. What will be your biggest obstacle in doing so?

3. What kind of help will you need?

4. Soul Exercise: Contact the person you think you might be able to help and set up a time to talk about forming a discipleship relationship with them. Before

you meet with them, consider what questions you think they might ask? How would you answer them?

Appendix B - New Testament Kingdom References

Matthew 3:1-2	Mark 1:14-15	Luke 22:28-30
Matthew 4:17	Mark 4:3-9	Luke 23:42-43
Matthew 4:23	Mark 4:11-12	
Matthew 5:3-10	Mark 4:13-20	
Matthew 5:19-20	Mark 4:26-29	John 3:3
Matthew 6:9-13	Mark 4:30-32	John 3:5
Matthew 6:33	Mark 10:14-16	John 18:37
Matthew 7:13-14	Mark 10:23-27	
Matthew 7:21	Mark 11:9-10	Acts 19:8
Matthew 8:11-12	Mark 12:32-34	Acts 28:23
Matthew 9:35	Mark 14:25	Acts 28:30-31
Matthew 10:5-7	Mark 15:42-43	
Matthew 11:11-12		
Matthew 12:28		Romans 14:17-19
Matthew 13:3-9	Luke 1:30-33	
Matthew 13:11-12	Luke 4:43	
Matthew 13:18-23	Luke 6:20-21	1 Corinthians 4:20
Matthew 13:24-30	Luke 7:28	1 Corinthians 6:9-11

Matthew 13:31-32	Luke 8:1	1 Corinthians 15:24-26
Matthew 13:33	Luke 8:4-15	1 Corinthians 15:50
Matthew 13:37-43	Luke 9:1-2	
Matthew 13:44-46	Luke 9:10-11	
Matthew 13:47-50	Luke 9:27	Ephesians 5:5
Matthew 13:52	Luke 9:60	
Matthew 16:16-19	Luke 9:62	
Matthew 16:26-28	Luke 10:9-12	Colossians 1:13-14
Matthew 18:1-4	Luke 11:2-4	Colossians 4:11
Matthew 18:23-35	Luke 11:20-22	
Matthew 19:11-12	Luke 11:52	
Matthew 19:13-15	Luke 12:31-32	1 Thessalonians 2:12
Matthew 19:23-24	Luke 13:18-19	2 Thessalonians 1:5-6
Matthew 20:1-16	Luke 13:20-21	
Matthew 20:20-21	Luke 13:22-30	
Matthew 21:28-32	Luke 14:15-24	2 Timothy 4:1
Matthew 21:33-44	Luke 16:16-17	2 Timothy 4:18
Matthew 22:1-14	Luke 17:20-21	
Matthew 23:13	Luke 18:16-17	
Matthew 24:14	Luke 18:24-30	Hebrews 12:28-29
Matthew 25:1-13	Luke 19:11-27	
Matthew 25:14-30	Luke 21:29-33	
Matthew 25:31-46	Luke 22:14-18	2 Peter 1:10-11

Appendix C - Resources to Go Further

I've included a few really good books here. If you aren't sure which one might be best for you, try one with a **bold** title!

Christian Beliefs: Twenty Basics Every Christian Should Know by Wayne Grudem. The title says it all: This book is a summary of twenty foundational beliefs of the Christian faith.

Devotional Classics by Richard Foster and James Bryan Smith. This is a great way to read and wrestle with some of the writings of people such as C.S. Lewis, Jonathan Edwards, St. Augustine, and John Calvin.

Forgotten God by Francis Chan. This will help you get to know the Holy Spirit and understand His role on the narrow way.

The Good and Beautiful God, Life, & Community by James Bryan Smith. This series of books will help train you to have the mind, character, and life of Christ.

The Knowledge of the Holy by A.W. Tozer. This timeless classic will help cement the true picture of God in your mind.

The Life You've Always Wanted by John Ortberg. This is an excellent introduction to some of the most basic and important soul exercises.

Multiply by Francis Chan. This summary of the Christian faith and practice includes excellent overviews of the Old and New Testaments.

The Practice of the Presence of God by Brother Lawrence. This short book records the wisdom and teachings of a 17th century monk as he learns to develop an everyday awareness of the presence of God.

The *Principle of the Path* by Andy Stanley. A quick but important reminder that we always end up where we are headed!

Prodigal God by Timothy Keller. This retelling of the prodigal Son story will challenge your notion of God's love for you and the people in your life.

A Quest for More: Living for Something Bigger than You by Paul David Tripp. Simply put, I have never seen a clearer description of the difference between living in the Kingdom of God and the kingdom of self.

Sacred Rhythms by Ruth Haley Barton. A book about soul exercises. Appendix C has a guide to choosing the appropriate spiritual discipline to practice.

A Shepherd Looks at Psalm 23 by W. Phillip Keller. An in-depth, illuminating walk through one of the most read Psalms of all time.

Soul Keeping by John Ortberg. A fantastic primer on the role and care of the most important part about you: your soul.

Strengthening the Soul of Your Leadership by Ruth Haley Barton. Essential spiritual formation principles and practices for leaders.

An Unhurried Life by Alan Fadling. Our culture is in a constant state of hurry. This book will help you recognize the hurry in your life and find freedom from it.

What Is the Gospel? by Greg Gilbert. This is a short, simple (and necessary) reminder of the message and the power of the Gospel.

Who I Am in Christ by Neil Anderson. This devotional book has 36 short chapters packed full of the truths about one of the most important yet elusive narratives we must believe: Who we are in Christ.

Acknowledgements

My wife Michele and my sons Adam and Isaac are without question the most fantastic family a man could ever have. They laugh with me, serve with me, encourage me, and challenge me in ways they are probably unaware of. Thank you for your continuous encouragement to do many things in life, including writing this book.

Terry Lewis has patiently endured my ramblings about discipleship over many years. All the while, he encouraged me to keep pushing ahead, always believing that God was working in me. Thank you for being my pastor and my friend.

I never met him personally, but I've read his books and heard him speak. I feel a profound sense of gratitude to Dallas Willard not only for talking about how to experience eternal life with Jesus but being a living, breathing example of that life to me and to so many others.

End Notes

[1] Chambers, Oswald. *My Utmost for His Highest*, Oswald Chambers Publication Association. Entry for March 13th.

[2] Willard, Dallas (2009-10-13). *The Great Omission* (Kindle Locations 277-279). HarperCollins. Kindle Edition.

[3] http://www.relevantmagazine.com/god/were-called-make-disciples-not-converts#juf5FlQ2dieE4Dy5.99

[4] Keller, Timothy. *The Prodigal God*. New York, NY: Penguin Group, 2008. Page 115.

[5] Willard, Dallas (2011-12-21). Renovation of the Heart: Putting on the Character of Christ with Bonus Content (Designed for Influence) (p. 85). Navpress. Kindle Edition.

[6] Tripp, Paul David (2007-10-31). A Quest for More: Living for Something Bigger than You (Kindle Locations 39-40). New Growth Press. Kindle Edition.

[7] Tripp, Paul David (2007-10-31). A Quest for More: Living for Something Bigger than You (Kindle Locations 1545-1547). New Growth Press. Kindle Edition.

[8] Tozer, A.W. (2012-08-12). *The Knowledge of the Holy* (p. 1). Fig. Kindle Edition.

[9] Ruth Haley Barton. *Sacred Rhythms: Arranging Our Lives for Spiritual Transformation* (Kindle Locations 222-226). Kindle Edition.

[10] Barry, John D., and Rebecca Kruyswijk. *Connect the*

Testaments: A One-Year Daily Devotional with Bible Reading Plan. Bellingham, WA: Lexham Press, 2012. Entry for February 6th.

[11] Keller, Phillip W. *A Shepherd Looks at Psalm 23*. Grand Rapids, MI: Zondervan Publishing House, 2007. Page 26.

[12] Keller, Phillip W. *A Shepherd Looks at Psalm 23*. Grand Rapids, MI: Zondervan Publishing House, 2007. Page 52.

[13] Francis Chan. *Forgotten God: Reversing Our Tragic Neglect of the Holy Spirit* (p. 17). Kindle Edition.

[14] Foster, Marilynne. *Tozer on the Holy Spirit*, 2000, Zur Ltd. Entry for April 1st

[15] Ortberg, John (2009-05-18). *The Life You've Always Wanted: Spiritual Disciplines for Ordinary People* (p. 26). Zondervan. Kindle Edition.

[16] Fadling, Alan (2013-03-07). *An Unhurried Life: Following Jesus' Rhythms of Work and Rest* (p. 160). InterVarsity Press. Kindle Edition.

[17] Ortberg, John (2009-05-18). *The Life You've Always Wanted: Spiritual Disciplines for Ordinary People* (p. 14). Zondervan. Kindle Edition.

[18] Keller, Phillip W. *A Shepherd Looks at Psalm 23*. Grand Rapids, MI: Zondervan Publishing House, 2007. Page 55.

[19] Chambers, Oswald. *My Utmost for His Highest*, Oswald Chambers Publication Association. Entry for February 24th

[20] Gaebelein, Frank E., Merrill C. Tenney, and Richard N. Longenecker. *The Expositor's Bible Commentary: John and Acts*. Vol. 9. Grand Rapids, MI: Zondervan Publishing House, 1981. Entry for John 15:5.

[21] Willard, Dallas (2009-10-13). *The Great Omission* (Kindle Locations 2450-2453). HarperCollins. Kindle Edition.

[22] Smith, James Bryan (2009-12-14). *The Good and Beautiful God: Falling in Love with the God Jesus Knows* (The Apprentice Series) (p. 25). IVP Books. Kindle Edition.

[23] Chambers, Oswald. *My Utmost for His Highest*, Oswald Chambers Publication Association, Entry for March 8th.

[24] James Bryan Smith. *The Good and Beautiful Life: Putting on the Character of Christ* (pp. 147-148). Kindle Edition.

[25] Ortberg, John (2009-05-18). *The Life You've Always Wanted: Spiritual Disciplines for Ordinary People* (p. 44). Zondervan. Kindle Edition.

[26] Tim Morey, *Embodying Our Faith* (Downers Grove, IL: InterVarsity Press, 2009), p. 111.

[27] Willard, Dallas (2009-10-13). *The Great Omission* (Kindle Locations 1315-1317). HarperCollins. Kindle Edition.

[28] Keller, Timothy. *The Prodigal God.* New York, NY: Penguin Group, 2008. Page 126.

[29] Craig Dykstra and Dorothy C. Bass, "Times of Yearning, Practices of Faith" in *Practicing our Faith* (San Francisco: Jossey- Bass, 1997), p. 5.

[30] James Bryan Smith. *The Good and Beautiful Community: Following the Spirit, Extending Grace, Demonstrating Love* (Kindle Locations 2000-2001). Kindle Edition.

[31] Ortberg, John (2014-04-22). *Soul Keeping: Caring For the Most Important Part of You* (p. 179). Zondervan. Kindle Edition.

[32] Stanley, Andy (2009-03-31). *The Principle of the Path: How to Get from Where You Are to Where You Want to Be* (p. 15). Thomas Nelson - A. Kindle Edition.

[33] Ortberg, John (2009-05-18). *The Life You've Always Wanted: Spiritual Disciplines for Ordinary People* (p. 53). Zondervan. Kindle Edition.

[34] Hybels, Bill (2014-08-19). *Simplify: Ten Practices to Unclutter Your Soul* (p. 50). Tyndale Momentum. Kindle Edition.

[35] Fadling, Alan (2013-03-07). *An Unhurried Life: Following Jesus' Rhythms of Work and Rest* (pp. 160-161). InterVarsity Press. Kindle Edition.

Made in the USA
Middletown, DE
02 August 2015